Other

The Honeymoon Album

^

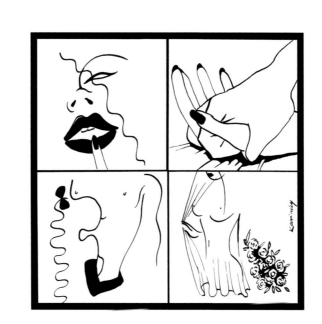

Kasia Karpinska-Sikorska

AuthorHouse™ UK
1663 Liberty Drive
Bloomington, IN 47403 USA
www.authorhouse.co.uk
Phone: 0800.197.4150

Published by AuthorHouse 07/19/2018

ISBN: 978-1-5462-8616-5 (sc)
ISBN: 978-1-5462-8615-8 (e)

Print information available on the last page.

author**HOUSE**®

Looks like royal approval for our book!

Acknowledgements

I wanted to come up with something unique! An idea or concept that hadn't been seen before. I had hoped that I would create something that met a need and would be useful to some. Unique, in business is supposed to be a good thing, a competitive advantage, but it appears it can also be a curse. So many potential investors were put off because they had nothing to compare my book with. The result. I had to turn to family for support, both emotional and financial to get my book into print.

So I acknowledge my family for their utterly insane backing!

Henry Winkler once said "Assumptions are the termites of relationships." Communication is a re-occurring theme in this book and this is no co-incidence. Every relationship, both inside the bedroom and outside will fail if we don't communicate with one another effectively. This book gives you a fun opportunity to be open and honest with each other. Put in the work at the beginning of the relationship and reap the rewards over many, many happy years that follow.

Dedication

For my family who have kept faith and continue to support my passions.

The (Other) Honeymoon Album
A newly-weds guide to a spanking good honeymoon

What's the point of this album?

- Stags & Hens get to challenge the honeymooning couple to play all kinds of games and sexy activities—space is provided—identify what you want one or both to do and leave your name, so they know who to thank later!

- It's a funny way of recording the most intimate details of a couples union.

- It can be used to inspire fun inside (and outside) the bedroom during the honeymoon AND becomes a permanent point of reference to look back on during the marriage.

- It can be an exciting way to kick start more play in the years ahead.

How is the album supposed to be used?

- The album has been set out to introduce a couple to each others bodies, sensuality and sexuality, progressively moving them to ever more intimate and naughtier places.

- In the 21st Century most couples are likely to have some understanding of one an others preferences so may opt to jump around the album selecting play ideas that they know will please each other.

- The 'games & challenges' give couples the chance to explore the content in a slightly different way and adds another layer of excitement to the play.

What is a 'Safe Word' and what is it used for?

- There are lots of opportunities in this album to push beyond what a couple might be traditionally comfortable doing. However much we think we might enjoy something the reality might not meet our expectation and we need to stop. A Safe Word gives each person control through out the play activities. As soon as the Safe Word is used the play stops. We have deliberately created a space on the next page to write down your Safe Word(s).

Legality!

- The album is all about play and fun. All activities must be consensual and comply with the law! This is very important if you are honeymooning abroad as some countries and cultures are less tolerant than others!

The newly-weds

Honeymoon

Dates:_____

Location:_____

Bride:

_____

Groom:

_____

Safe word:

_____

Safe word:

_____

The (other) Honeymoon Album has been gifted to you with the malevolent love and best wishes of the following degenerates masquerading as friends:

PS These are also the thoughtful and fun loving souls who have taken the time and effort to challenge you to participate in a number of activities through out this book you may, or may not, have ever considered trying before. It is for you, the happy couple, to think of a system of rewards and forfeits eg money; meals; drinks; shopping spree's or confessions for challenges accepted or refused!

Contents

Equipment check

Here are a few suggestions for each activity. Please feel free to amend the lists to suit yourselves.

Activity one: Exploring each other

Just requires a slow, gentle touch. Be inquisitive about all areas of the body.

Activity two: Dressing up

While your home can look like a costume rental shop on honeymoon you are going to need to be more creative. In addition to lingerie try selecting items from your wardrobe that have a practical use but can double up as something naughty eg plaid skirt for school uniform; white shirt/blouse for room service; a tie for bondage and role play characters etc.

Activity three: Positions

Please remember that some positions require a level of dexterity and flexibility that is not possessed by all—avoid injury with a liberal application of common sense!

The hotel should provide additional pillows to support adventurous play. Otherwise, you should be good to go!

Activity four: Sploshing

Most of your needs can be met at a local supermarket: Cream; honey; cake; jelly; sweet and savoury sauces NB Try for a range of sensations taste—sweet & savoury/hot & cold and texture too. Good moment to check if your partner has any food allergies—not the kind of swelling we are looking for!

Activity five: The guessing game

Phallic objects and items that can be rolled across sensitive areas. Think about textures and think about temperature too. Some items can be purchased locally from a supermarket eg courgettes, carrots & grapes. Others, like your favourite dildo or hair brush need to be packed in advance!

Equipment check continued...

Activity six: Introduction to BDSM
Packing is all about getting creative with space. Take items that have more than one use eg ties; stockings; tights. Take advantage of items that you know are going to be where you are staying eg pillow cases as gags or blindfolds; hotel Welcome Folder for spanking! This leaves more room for the specialist items like whips, clamps and plugs!

Activity seven: Sensual massage
Make the best of what you've got: Sun cream and sun lotion. Baby oil or KY jelly. Alternatively, there are many different options of specialist massage oil. You may want to put a towel down on whatever surface you are going to perform the massage to protect it from the oils! In addition, It is always worth packing these items in plastic cooler bags to prevent spillage in your suitcase. If you are combining massage with Sploshing try and remember which oils can be digested and which cannot!

Activity eight: Role play
In Activity Two we talk about packing items of clothing that
can double as every day wear and play wear.
Packing some props won't take up too much room in the suitcase but can make a big difference to the role play. For example, name badges from any stationer for room service & conference role plays.
If your partner has a favourite role play that requires a uniform then why
not indulge them—pack it secretly— riot police helmet and shield might
be difficult to accommodate but effort is usually rewarded!
Avoid packing anything that looks like a weapon!!

Activity nine: I Dare You
We've provided you with some dares to 'get you going' and hopefully friends have added something naughty too! The Dare Game can be huge fun on your honeymoon and through out your marriage. To maximise the fun try not to get arrested—remember different countries and cultures have different laws, tolerance and sense of humour!
Dares should escalate like foreplay, building in naughtiness and intensity—the points are a clue but you know your partner best—use easier dares to begin with so they become more confident and, hopefully, more willing to have a go at the naughtier ones.

A guide to............Exploring each other

EARS: Gentle caresses using finger tips; lips with soft nibbling; tip of the penis; erect nipples; the tongue. Whisper naughty things—at the beginning, during foreplay, keep it sensual—language should build suspense toward a crescendo.

THIGHS: Before visiting his penis or her vagina the thighs represent the last chance to tease your partner. Whether using your fingers, tongue or both, by the time you reach their genitals you want your partner ready to explode! The thighs are your cue to slow down, take your time, linger! You can throw in some dirty talk "What do you want?" "Tell me what you want me to do to you?" - you get the idea, it's all about anticipation.

Name Of challenger	Name(s) Of those challenged	The challenge

A guide to............**Exploring each other**

FEET: Foot fetishes are very common but you don't need to be a fetishist to have fun with feet. Some people are very self conscious of their feet and so having someone else give them attention can be a real turn off— communicate with your partner! Fun can involve tonguing; sucking; massage & foot masturbation.

FINGERS: Fingers & toes contain lots of nerve endings that crave their own attention— responding very well to massage & sucking.

NIPPLES: A woman's nipples tend to be more sensitive than a mans but erotic play can be pleasurable for both sexes. Some people like rough play with nipples but if you don't know what your partners preference is then start gently and see how far they want to go— communicate! Fingers; lips; tongue; penis; vagina. Remember the art of teasing is to start on the outer breast and work in toward the nipples — building anticipation!

Name Of challenger	Name(s) Of those challenged	The challenge

A guide to............Exploring each other

NECK: Often neglected erogenous zone! Excellent place to get things started beyond the initial kiss. Fingers, lips, tongue, caressing & massaging—keep it gentle. Don't worry about the giggles—it's supposed to be fun!

TESTICLES: Be gentle! Build your action when cupping with the hand, using fingers and nails. Tongue & mouth should also start gently—what you see on the internet is not a good starting point! If he is not fully erect—the balls are a great place to start, building the excitement before moving onto the penis.

PERINEUM: At this point in the book we are not suggesting anal sex—although if that is where it ends up who are we to deny consenting adults! Caressing, kissing and massaging the buttocks moving in toward the perineum gives your partner time to decide how far they want to go! The anus should be penetrated slowly & carefully whatever you are using! A good quality lubricant (non-petroleum if you are using a condom at any point) can help if you are using anything longer or harder than your tongue!

Name Of challenger	Name(s) Of those challenged	The challenge

*A guide to............***Exploring each other**

VAGINA: Literally time to unfold the mystery! You need to know your way around your partners vagina. i-net search engine to find: Mons; labia, vulva, clitoris, urethra and vagina.—do your homework and don't assume she knows! The clitoris is the most sensitive area so work towards it. If you tease successfully, she will tell you in no uncertain terms when she wants you to work on her clitoris. Good communication over time will let you know exactly how to satisfy her.

PENIS: The most sensitive area tends to be on the underside at the end of the shaft where it meets the purple head. Tease towards this spot using fingers, tongue, lips etc The purple head itself is very sensitive so again think about building toward these areas with fingers, nails (carefully), lips & tongue. Lubricants can be helpful but not to everyone's taste! Your own saliva will reduce friction. Try sucking an extra strong mint just before oral sex!

Name Of challenger	Name(s) Of those challenged	The challenge

A *record of*............**Exploring Each Other**

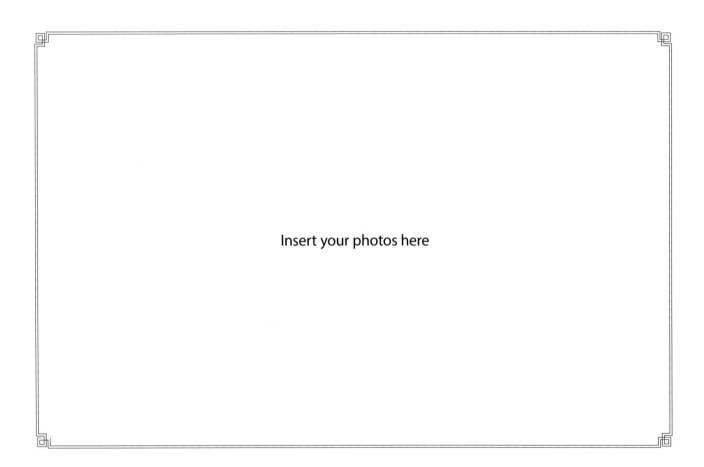

Insert your photos here

A guide to............Dressing Up

Dressing up should be fun for both of you and provides an opportunity to explore and combine with activities like sploshing, role-play or dares!

Call a professional. Have an escort delivered to the door or pick her up in the bar. Lots of little accessories are available to create the escort, lap-dancer or stripper!

Packing the whole gown might not be practical but the veil & lingerie give you the opportunity to relive the magic of the first night or conjure up naughty fantasies

Name Of challenger	Name(s) Of those challenged	The challenge

A guide to............Dressing Up

Re-define what is meant by room service. Sub-dom role play or the you bump into the maid while getting out of the shower.

Someone's broken the law and needs to be punished! Put them in handcuffs and make them pay for their crimes!

Lingerie and accessories can spice up any encounter. How much are you willing to show off? Does your partner have a special outfit they like - secretly pack it?

Name Of challenger	Name(s) Of those challenged	The challenge

A guide to............Dressing Up

Fetish wear...Go on, give it a go! The texture, the restricted movement, the wipe clean surface - all excellent reasons to let go of your inhibitions!

Have you been summoned to the teachers office to receive a reward or a punishment? Can the inscrutable teacher be seduced?

Bed bath, rectal exam or cough & drop.
The naughty nurse is one of the most enduring fantasies

Name Of challenger	Name(s) Of those challenged	The challenge

A guide to............Dressing Up

Sub or Dom, secretary or boss. This outfit is easy to put together and versatile as part of your wider honeymoon wardrobe.

Whether dealing with red hot fire or rescuing an abandoned pussy, the fireman and his hose is always a winner!

Cuffed and brutalised by a bad cop...
A very bad cop who knows how to use her hand-cuffs and a night-stick!

Name Of challenger	Name(s) Of those challenged	The challenge

A guide to............**Dressing Up**

Leave the surgery to surgeons but that still leaves a large number of examinations possible for an active imagination!

Military uniform can be a huge turn on. Pick a service, pick a scenario and let war commence. Word of caution, anything resembling a weapon in luggage is unwise!

A navy costume is created here with a dress and homemade accessories. Use your imaginations and save a fortune in expensive outfits!

Name Of challenger	Name(s) Of those challenged	The challenge

A *record of*............**Dressing Up**

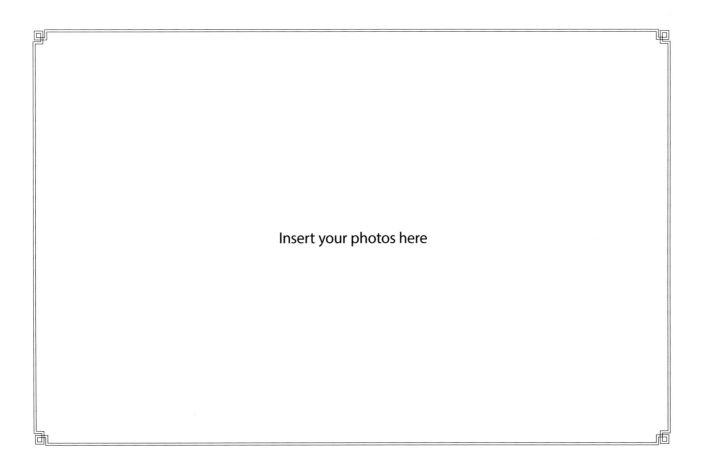

Insert your photos here

A *record of*............**Dressing Up**

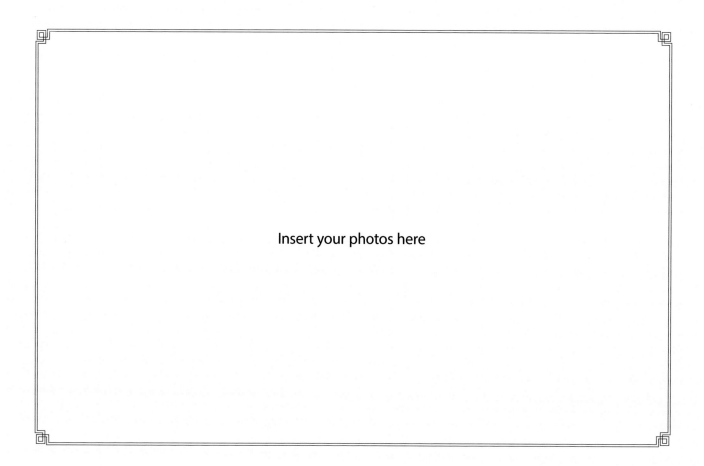

Insert your photos here

A guide to...........Positions

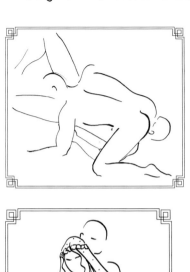

Twin Towers

Union

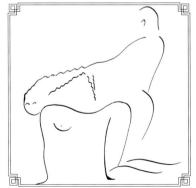

Bad Little Doggie

Name Of challenger	Name(s) Of those challenged	The challenge

A guide to............Positions

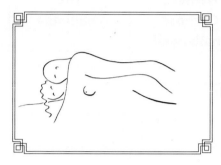

**Broken
Star Fish**

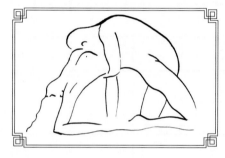

**Entering
The Bridge**

Missionary

Name Of challenger	Name(s) Of those challenged	The challenge

A guide to............Positions

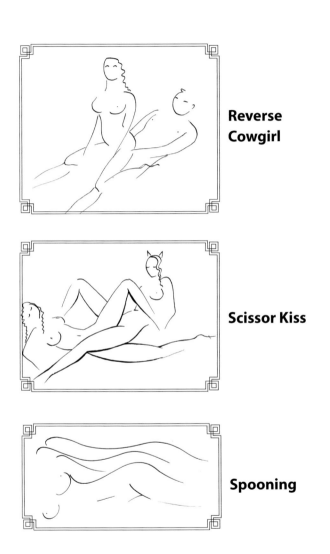

Reverse Cowgirl

Scissor Kiss

Spooning

Name Of challenger	Name(s) Of those challenged	The challenge

A guide to............Positions

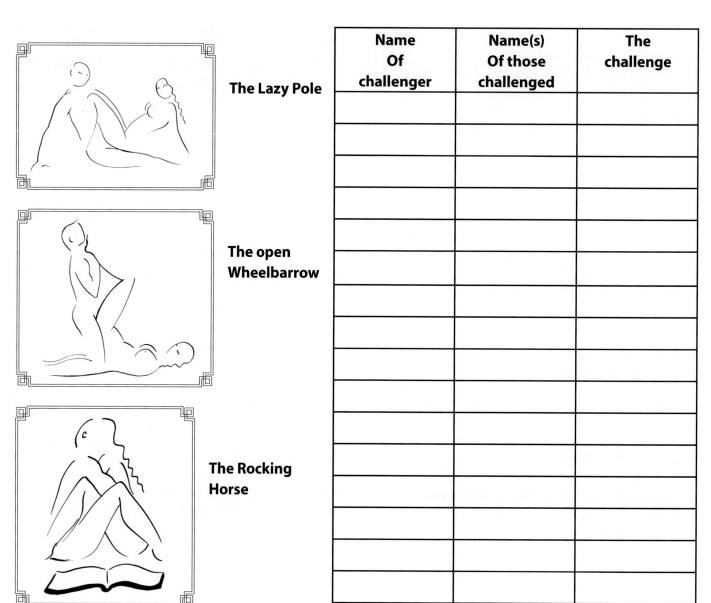

The Lazy Pole

The open Wheelbarrow

The Rocking Horse

Name Of challenger	Name(s) Of those challenged	The challenge

A *record of*............**Positions**

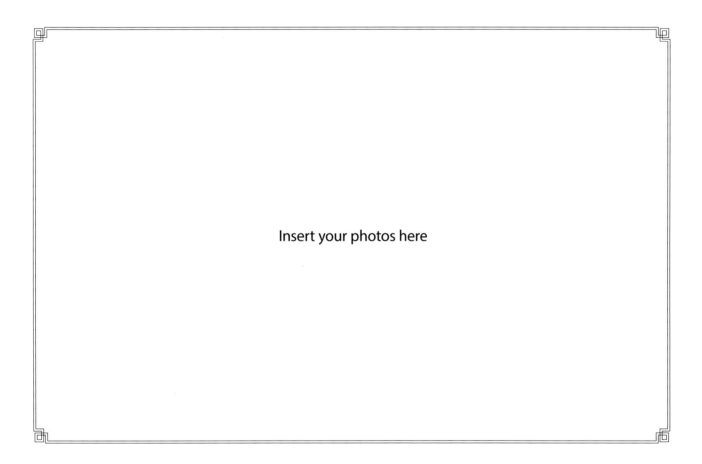

Insert your photos here

A record of………...**Positions**

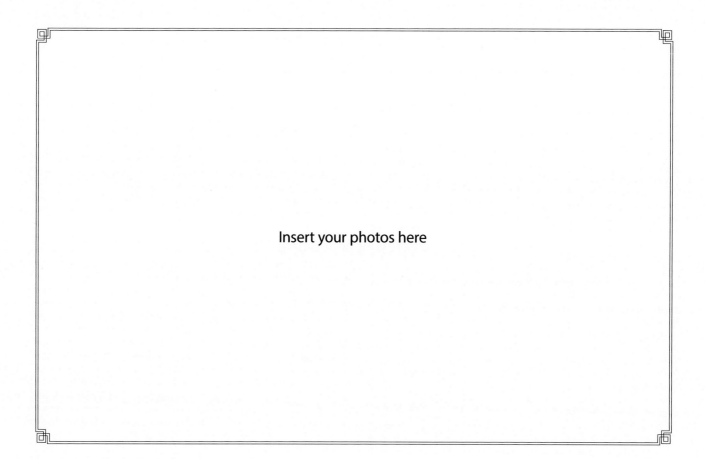

Insert your photos here

A guide to............**Sploshing**

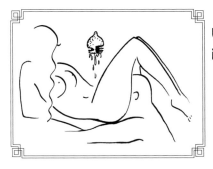

Using fresh ingredients

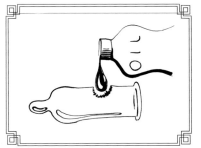

Beware of petroleum oils

Having fun with food

Name Of challenger	Name(s) Of those challenged	The challenge

A guide to............Sploshing

Layering food combinations

Not everything goes with pubic hair

Sharing the feast

Name Of challenger	Name(s) Of those challenged	The challenge

A guide to...........**Sploshing**

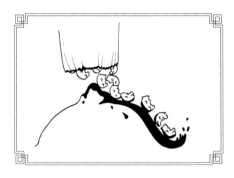

Sweet & Sour

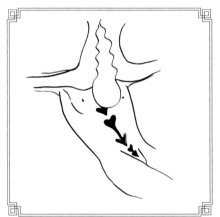

Teasing

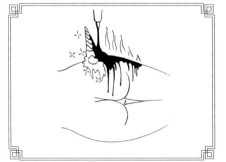

Using hot and cold

Name Of challenger	Name(s) Of those challenged	The challenge

A guide to............**Sploshing**

Allergies

This book above all others should contain a warning & a joke about allergies to nuts, I'm just not sure what it should be!

Name Of challenger	Name(s) Of those challenged	The challenge

A record of............**Sploshing**

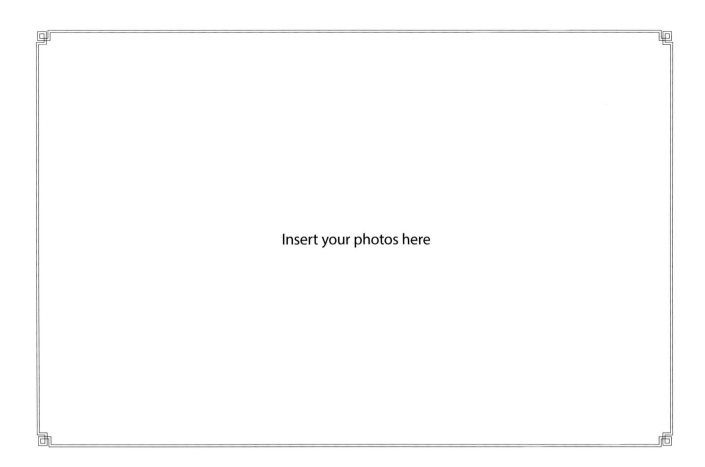

Insert your photos here

A *record of*............**Sploshing**

Insert your photos here

A guide to............The guessing game

The guessing game is an excellent starting place for blending activities. Your partner needs to be blindfolded and tied to prevent them interfering with your actions but also to heighten excitement by making them vulnerable. In this position you can experiment with different objects on/in different areas of their body.

Your partner must try and guess what objects you are using!

A correct guess can be rewarded while an incorrect guess can be punished. These should be agreed before hand and are limited only by your imagination! Rewards and forfeits could be linked to other activities in this book and/or could relate to the everyday—whether you get a desert at dinner, your favourite cocktail or who gets to dress you in the morning, can you have fun applying the sun block in public how touchy feely can you get at the bar etc!

You can organise the giving of these rewards and punishments through out the honeymoon to help maintain a constant state of sexiness and arousal. Continued…

Name Of challenger	Name(s) Of those challenged	The challenge

A guide to.............The guessing game

When selecting objects think about the order you want to use them and how and where you want to use them. You are always trying to build excitement to a crescendo. Think about the size of the objects, their texture and whether they are hot or cold. Hopefully during Activity One: Exploring each other you have become familiar with your partners most sensitive erogenous zones and can now exploit that knowledge to stimulate them fully.

Objects like vibrators, dildos and plugs might be packed especially but re-member other objects like hair brushes, lipsticks and make up brushes are probably being packed anyway. Other items, particularly perishable goods, can be purchased from the nearest supermarket. Most fruit and veg sections will contain items that can be used to caress as well as penetrate.

If your room has a mini bar take advantage of the opportunity to chill some objects. If you heating anything be careful not to burn your partner, remember you are likely to be applying product to an already sensitive area! A&E staff have endless anecdotes about bizarre objects removed from strange places, to avoid becoming the latest "You'll never guess what I saw today!" story, apply a liberal amount of common sense to your play!

Name Of challenger	Name(s) Of those challenged	The challenge

A record of............**The Guessing Game**

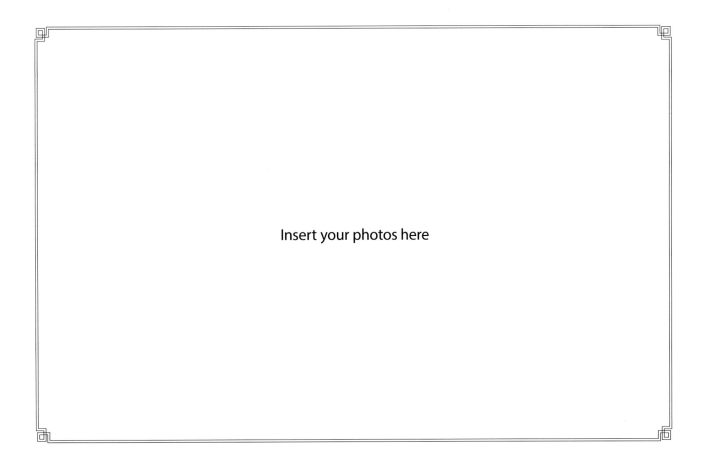

Insert your photos here

A record of............**The Guessing Game**

Insert your photos here

An introductory guide to...**BDSM**

As Bondage Discipline Sadism Masochism (BDSM) has infiltrated popular culture through books, television and film, many people are now willing to give it a go! Elaborate dungeons and degrees in knot tying are no longer necessary to have a bit of fun with BDSM. Expensive specialist kit is not necessary to get started. We'll make all kinds of suggestions later on here but, to be honest, you can get started with a scarf, a couple of pairs of tights, an imagination and a sense of humour! Oh, don't forget the 'safe words'.

You can share the same safe word as your partner or have one each. The important thing is that you're both clear what the safe word is and that it means STOP. Why use a safe word? Part of the fun of being spanked, for example, is pleading with you partner to stop while really wanting it to continue. At some point, however, you might actually want the spanking to stop. In order for your partner to know when play time is really over shouting the pre-arranged safe word leaves them in no doubt they must stop. The safe word needs to be a word you would not normally use in this context eg wheel barrow or dust bin.

Name Of challenger	Name(s) Of those challenged	The challenge

An introductory guide to...**BDSM**

If the fear of having to explain pink fluffy hand cuffs to airport security is too much for you, don't panic, two pairs of tights/stockings (min) can secure your partner so they are suitably vulnerable. More tights or a scarf also make an excellent blindfold. Having restrained your partner you might want to inflict punishment and for this canes, whips and paddles are ideal but if you're not sure whether airport security might confiscate them, never fear, there are alternatives! Lots of hotels have table tennis where paddles can be rented or acquired with a small deposit. So long as you return them they are not likely to ask why you weren't seen using them.

An additional kink is then watching other guests subsequently using the paddles knowing what you have just done with them! If there's no table tennis you can go 'old school' and spank your partner with the palm of your hand or use a trouser belt or rolled magazine, hotel brochure, newspaper or the sacrilegious among you could use the copy of the Bible placed in lots of hotel rooms! Twisted towels can be used to flick the buttocks or the more hard core might check the wardrobe for wire coat-hangers!

Name Of challenger	Name(s) Of those challenged	The challenge

An introductory guide to...**BDSM**

A bed without bed rails at head and foot should not deter those determined to have fun with BDSM. Tights are usually stretchy and so look for the feet of the bed and/or mattress handles. Why restrict yourself to the bed? Think laterally—or vertically and horizontally—if you can tie your partner to it, you can play! Word of caution: If a lot of wriggling is anticipated (and it should be, if you're doing it right) make sure whatever you have tied your partner to is not likely to collapse on them or you—that's probably too sadistic and/or masochistic!

You can cross reference your play with Activity One: Exploring each other; Activity Four: Sploshing and Activity Five: The guessing game.

Name Of challenger	Name(s) Of those challenged	The challenge

A record of............**BDSM**

Insert your photos here

A record of............**BDSM**

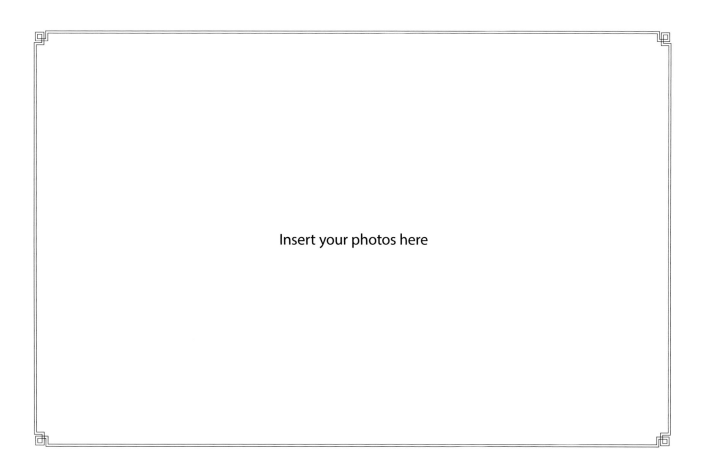

Insert your photos here

A guide to.........**Sensual Massage**

A lubricant helps with massage. If you have to you can use sun cream—it's something you're probably already planning to pack BUT if this is your thing sensual oils can't be beaten (unless you're combining this Activity with the last BDSM!). You can buy edible oils, particularly handy if you get a bit peckish and combine with Activity 4: Sploshing. Use a towel to avoid staining bedsheets etc

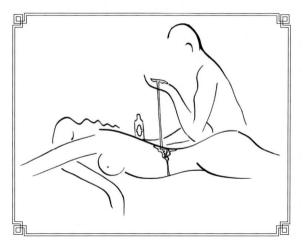

Essential Oils

Name Of challenger	Name(s) Of those challenged	The challenge

A guide to..........**Sensual Massage**

The hands and feet are a good starting place. Fetishists will already know that both areas are full of nerve endings that will appreciate firm attention particularly the palms and souls. Don't forget between the fingers and toes with a more gentle touch!

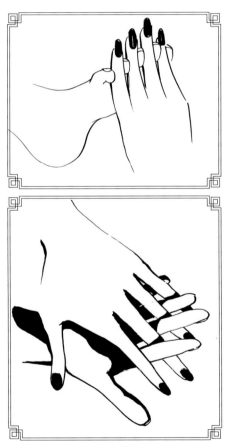

Name Of challenger	Name(s) Of those challenged	The challenge

A guide to..........Sensual Massage

The neck & ears are erogenous zones but are often neglected during foreplay and sensual massage. The neck is a particularly vulnerable area so must be treated with great care—use only gentle massage and try and avoid swirling movements. Follow the neck from the shoulders to the base of the skull, moving with muscle groups. Massaging the scalp is very relaxing but avoid oils that are likely to matt the hair. Perhaps start here and then move on—it also reduces the chance of putting your partner to sleep (unless that is your intention!!)

Name Of challenger	Name(s) Of those challenged	The challenge

A guide to..........**Sensual Massage**

The buttocks and thighs. You can be firm. Ideal place to practice your 'cupping' and 'karate kid' moves. Circle around the anus and move in close to the outer labia but avoid contact with both (at the early stages at least!)

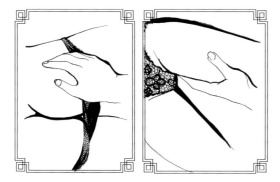

You can use all kinds of objects to help give a more intense sensual massage. You can create a very different sexual atmosphere by using different objects. Ie Feathers and silk create a very different vibe to a cane or abrasive substance!

Name Of challenger	Name(s) Of those challenged	The challenge

A guide to..........Sensual Massage

We have mentioned several time in this book that teasing is going to enhance both the element of fun and the sexual experience. Inner thighs, breasts, buttocks and the genitals should be the final destination of the tour of your partner's body!

The hip's. 'Smoothing' with the palms and 'stroking' with finger tips (and nails) are all good. To maintain the tease element of this Activity, avoid direct contact with the genitals.

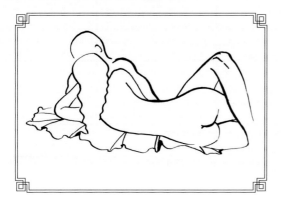

Name Of challenger	Name(s) Of those challenged	The challenge

A *record of*............**Sensual Massage**

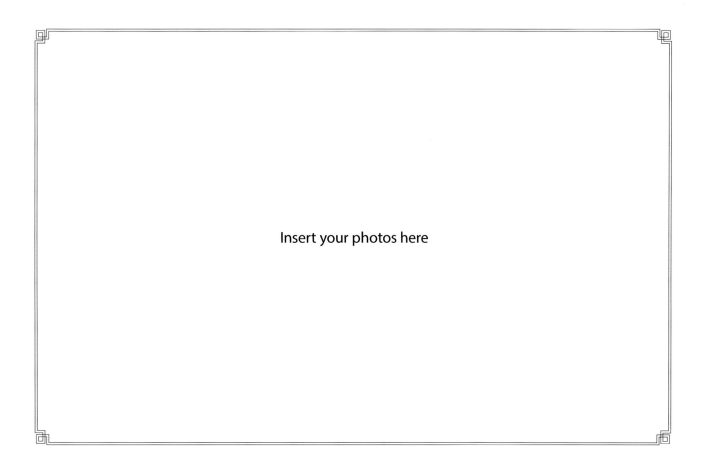

Insert your photos here

A record of............Sensual Massage

Insert your photos here

A guide to.......... **Role Play**

Room service:

Take it in turns delivering room service.

- No cash for a tip! How else can I thank you?
- Thats not the tip I wanted!
- You can eat what I've brought you or I'll eat anything you put in front of me!
- You want to pay with your ??? - that'll do nicely!"

The secret agent:

You can role play like Meryl Streep for an Oscar or you can go for the laughs, either way you're going to have fun with this classic.

- I'm taking a huge risk by talking to you but it's a matter of life or death!
- The name is Doe, John Doe!

Fun passwords

- My baguette is full of camembert!
- I need the cream licked from my mille foie!
- I need someone to polish my Aston!
- My weapon is in my pocket and its ready to go off!

Picked up in a bar:

Pre plan your roles then get stuck in. The more you commit to the role play the more fun you will have.

- Are you here for the sex toy conference?
- I do love my husband/wife but sometimes it is nice being away on business!
- I can't believe my bad luck, I'm on honeymoon and my partner is stuck in the room with a stomach bug!

The escort service:

There are male escorts in this world so there is no excuse, you can both have a go at being the escort as well as the client.

Your fantasy might be high class or street walker—make sure your partner knows what to pack or surprise them by packing it for them!

The escort can be pre booked to your room or you can 'pick them up' in the bar or on the street!

This could be a role play that allows your partner to do something they don't normally do! A 'special' act can be owned by this character and only performed when in character.

Be careful exchanging money in public—this can be sexy and you can get a thrill from being spotted but it might be safer to pass an empty envelope than have to explain a wad of notes to the hotel manager or local police!

A celebrity:

A lot of couples have an agreed list of celebs they would be ok their partner having sex with if the opportunity arose— usually because they know they are more likely to win the lottery than have their celebrity dream come true!

Here's the chance to take that fantasy one step further.

Think about how they might dress and what they might talk about eg their last album or film role.

Decide at the beginning of the role play if you are happy with your partner screaming their fantasy celebs name during sex!

Consensual sex:

"stop!" means stop and "No!" means no. However, if you use your safe word(s) as part of a mutually agreed role play, you can fulfil all kinds of consensual fantasies!

Other possible RP to think about:

- Age
- Interview
- Physical Appearance
- People you know

Other RP continued....

Remember to borrow or combine from other activities. For example, Activity Two: Dressing up.

- Police Officer
- Doctors & nurses
- Fireman
- Plumber
- Teacher
- Porn star

A word of advice:

Most honeymoon couples today are not exploring sex for the first time, so are likely to already have a good idea about each others fantasies, turn-on's and turn-off's. This means RP choices are not likely to shock the hell out of each other!

If you are new to each other and/or role play start in the shallow end with a generic fantasy about a nurse or police office before exploring the deepest, darkest recesses of your imagination!

A *record of* ....**Role Play**

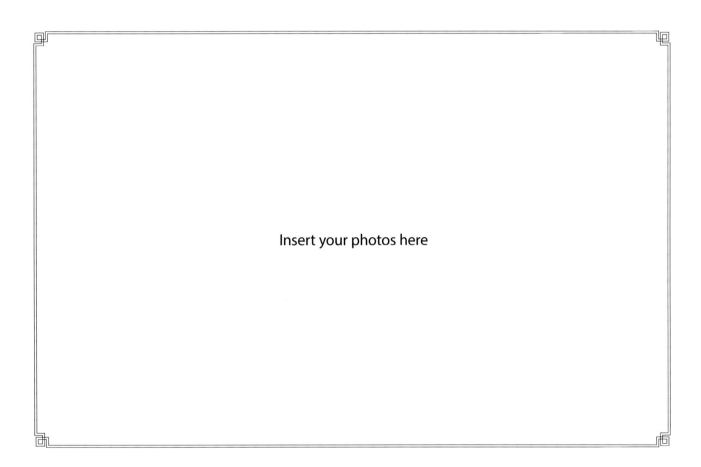

Insert your photos here

A record of............**Role Play**

Insert your photos here

A guide to..........I Dare You

The cards can be used in a number of different ways but, first cut them from the album. Decide where you are going to play 'Dares' - a bar, restaurant or club would be most appropriate. Divide the cards between you and your partner.

Game 1: Rapide.

In this version of the game you will take turns selecting a card. Each player must complete the task written on the card within 5 minutes. If they fail to complete the Dare or fail within the time limit they face a penalty. You could make this a drinking game with penalties paid in alcohol—the plus side here is the more you drink the less inhibited you become the more likely the dares will be completed! Decide the goal of the game ie most dares completed; most points scored—the winner gets to use their Prize Card.

Before the game starts you each write on the Prize Card what it is you want if you win: I get to pick tomorrows restaurant; You buy me the shoes I want; We try position X from Activity Three: Positions; I pick one of the dares you turned down. You can decide between you whether to show each other at the beginning of the game what you have chosen as a prize or whether to leave it as a surprise at the end of the game!

Name Of challenger	Name(s) Of those challenged	The challenge

A guide to..........I Dare You

The cards can be used in a number of different ways but, first cut them from the album. Decide where you are going to play 'Dares' - a bar, restaurant or club would be most appropriate. Divide the cards between you and your partner.

Game 2—The long game.

The Prize Cards are filled out at the beginning of the game. The Dare Cards are shuffled and distributed but this time you can see the Dare Cards you have been dealt. During the 'play time' of the game: The whole day; evening or a specified time period, you can each play any of your cards at any time. You do not need to take it in turns. The idea is to play the perfect card at the perfect moment to maximise the sexiness and/or embarrassment of the dare.

In the event of a draw both Prize Cards are played—why miss out—any excuse to maximise the naughtiness!

NB Some countries have strict laws on public nudity and displays of affection. Have fun but be respectful of the laws and culture of the country you are guests in!

Name Of challenger	Name(s) Of those challenged	The challenge

Score page 1

BRIDE		GROOM	
Dare	Points	Dare	Points

Score page 2

BRIDE		GROOM	
Dare	Points	Dare	Points

Score page 3

BRIDE		GROOM	
Dare	**Points**	**Dare**	**Points**

Score page 4

BRIDE		GROOM	
Dare	**Points**	**Dare**	**Points**

I dare you *Dare and Prize Cards to cut out*

Remove an item of clothing in public = 1pt

OR

Let your partner choose the item of clothing to be removed = 3pts

---

Eat two items of food in a highly seductive way = 2pts

OR

Eat two items of food seductively while looking at your partners choice of stranger = 4pts

---

Dance with a total stranger = 5pts

OR

Dance provocatively with a total stranger = 8pts

Join a conversation with a group of strangers = 2pts

OR

Join the conversation with strangers and tell them a true intimate sex fact within 5 mins = 10pts

---

Kiss a total stranger on the lips = 5pts

OR

French kiss a total stranger = 10pts

Name Of challenger	Name(s) Of those challenged	The challenge

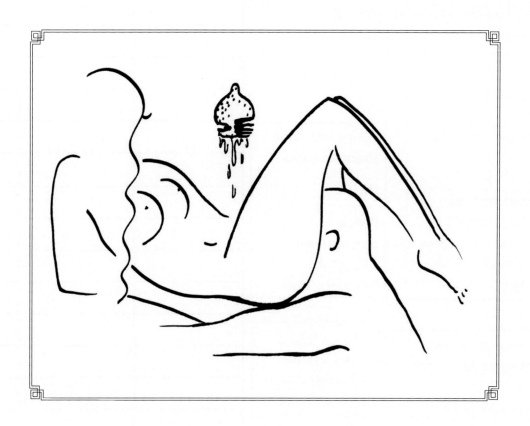

I dare you *Dare and Prize Cards to cut out*

Expose yourself to your partner (min 30 secs) = 5 pts

OR

Expose yourself to someone of your partners choosing.

Nipples = 5pts (each)

Genitals = 15pts

Remove your underwear = 2pts

OR

Remove your underwear in public = 5pts

Eat/drink something off your partners body

Hand/lips = 1pt

Another body part 2pts

Nipples = 5pts (each)

Genitals = 10pts

One minute to massage your partner. You can go close but you cannot touch their most intimate parts! = 3pts

OR

The last 20 secs are used to publicly caress your partners most intimate places = 10pts

---

Masturbate for 5 mins = 10pts

OR

Additional 10pts if you climax.

Perform oral sex on your partner for 30 seconds = 25pts

If you make them orgasm they lose 15pts

Name Of challenger	Name(s) Of those challenged	The challenge

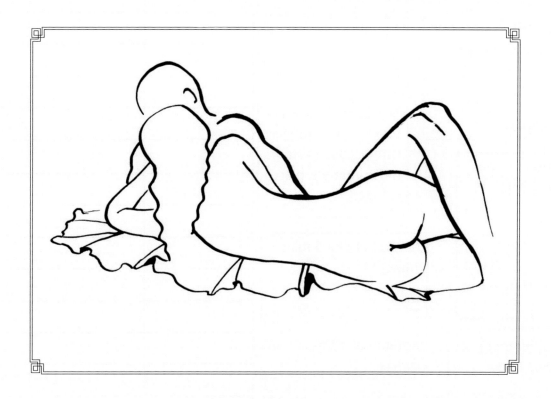

I dare you *Dare and Prize Cards to cut out*

Nibble, kiss and lick your partners ears/neck for min 1 minute = 3pts

---

Dry hump your partner = 3pts

OR

Your partner pick the body part you are humping = 10pts

Taste your partners sexual fluids = 10pts

Masturbate your partner for 5 mins = 15pts

If they orgasm, they lose 15pts

Insert a finger into your partners vagina or anus for 1 minute = 15pts

OR

The last 20 secs are used to publicly caress your partners most intimate places = 10pts

---

Masturbate a stranger = 50pts

Perform oral sex on a stranger = 100pts

Name Of challenger	Name(s) Of those challenged	The challenge

I dare you *Dare and Prize Cards to cut out*

One minute to massage your partner. You can go close but you cannot touch their most intimate parts! = 3pts

OR

The last 20 secs are used to publicly caress your partners most intimate places = 10pts

Masturbate for 5 mins = 10pts

OR

Additional 10pts if you climax.

Full sex with a stranger = 250pts

Perform oral sex on your partner for 30 seconds = 25pts

If you make them orgasm they lose 15pts

Name Of challenger	Name(s) Of those challenged	The challenge

PRIZE CARD
(Write your reward/forfeit here each game)

PRIZE CARD
(Write your reward/forfeit here each game)

PRIZE CARD
(Write your reward/forfeit here each game)

PRIZE CARD
(Write your reward/forfeit here each game)

PRIZE CARD
(Write your reward/forfeit here each game)

PRIZE CARD
(Write your reward/forfeit here each game)

PRIZE CARD
(Write your reward/forfeit here each game)

PRIZE CARD
(Write your reward/forfeit here each game)

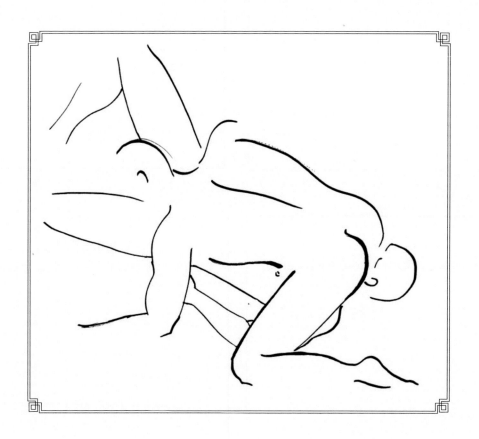

A *record of*............ **more fun!**

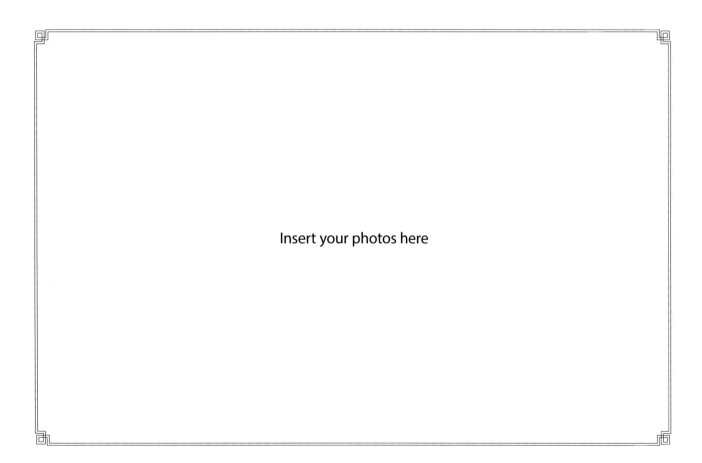

Insert your photos here

A record of............ **more fun!**

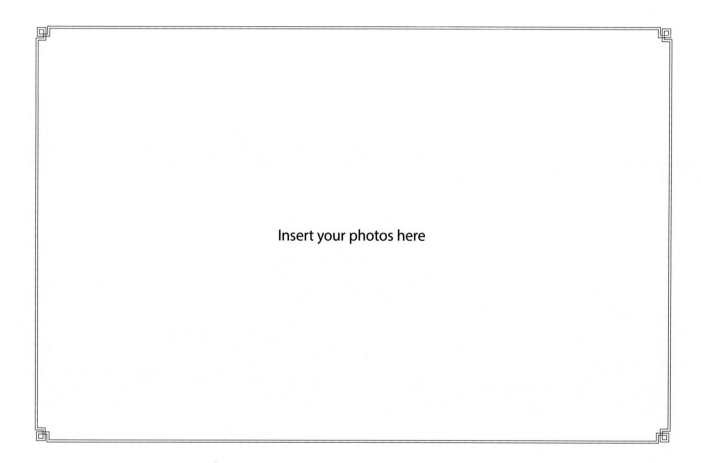

Insert your photos here

A record of............ **more fun!**

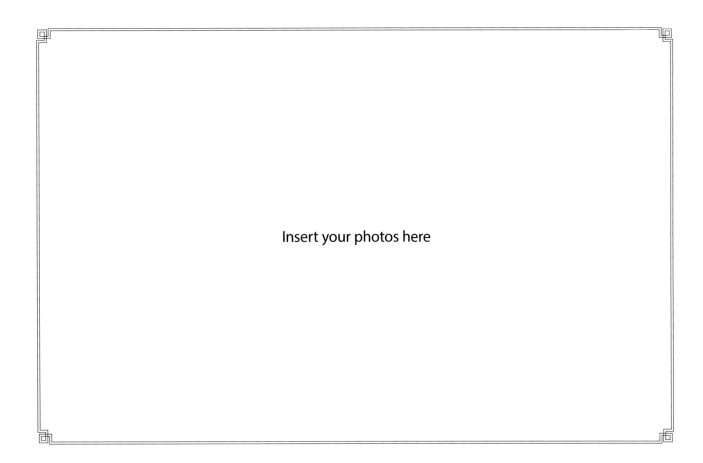

Insert your photos here

Kasia Karpinska-Sikorska was born in Lodz, Poland on 27th April 1980. Kasia graduated from the prestigious High School of Art in 2001 and went on to become a Master of Art History at the University of Lodz.

When married, Kasia and her photographer husband set-up Funnygames Redesign. Their studio produced a diverse range of exhibitions using a variety of eclectic media. As their brand became synonymous with ground breaking avante-garde work they moved to London to start a family and progress their work.

In the last couple of years, as her children grow-up, Kasia has been looking for a vehicle for her creativity. The (other) Honeymoon Album represents the outcome of two year's work pulling ideas and experiences together in what she now hopes is a successful format.

The book is a response to how so many friends have viewed their honeymoon as "just another holiday."

Art remains her first love and the artwork in the book is her own work and, like the book, blends humour and eroticism to provide an interesting read and even more interesting honeymoon!

Kasia's own reading habits covers philosophy, ancient, modern and post-modern art.

Printed in the United States
By Bookmasters